HAL LEONARD

UKULELE METHOD

Supplement to Any Ukulele Method

EASY SONGS FOR UKULELE

Play the Melodies of 20 Pop, Folk, Country, and Blues Songs

BY LIL' REV

To access audio visit:
www.halleonard.com/mylibrary

Enter Code
1460-0832-8849-8942

ISBN 978-1-4234-0276-3

HAL•LEONARD®
CORPORATION
7777 W. BLUEMOUND RD. P.O. BOX 13819 MILWAUKEE, WI 53213

Visit Hal Leonard Online at
www.halleonard.com

INTRODUCTION

Welcome to *Easy Songs for Ukulele*, a collection of 20 pop, folk, country, and blues favorites arranged for easy ukulele. If you're a beginning ukulele player, you've come to the right place; these well-known songs will have you playing, reading, and enjoying music in no time!

This collection can be used on its own or as a supplement to the *Hal Leonard Ukulele Method – Book One* or any other beginning ukulele method. The songs are arranged in order of difficulty. Each melody is presented in an easy-to-read format—including lyrics to help you follow along and ukulele chord diagrams for optional accompaniment. As you progress through the book, you can go back and try playing the chords as well. Additional lyrics are also provided at the end of many of the songs in case you want to sing extra verses.

USING THE AUDIO

Easy *Songs for Ukulele* is available as a book/audio package so you can practice playing with accompaniment. Each song begins with a full (or partial) measure of clicks, which sets the tempo and prepares you for playing along. To remove the ukulele from the mix, just pan your playback device all the way to the right using Playback+, so you only hear the guitar. To tune your ukulele to the audio, use the Tuning Notes.

SONG STRUCTURE

The songs in this book have different sections, which may or may not include the following:

Intro
This is usually a short instrumental section that "introduces" the song at the beginning.

Verse
This is one of the main sections of a song and conveys most of the storyline. A song usually has several verses, all with the same music but each with different lyrics.

Chorus
This is often the most memorable section of a song. Unlike the verse, the chorus usually has the same lyrics every time it repeats.

Bridge
This section is a break from the rest of the song, often having a very different chord progression and feel.

Solo
This is an instrumental section, often played over the verse or chorus structure.

Outro
Similar to an intro, this section brings the song to an end.

ENDINGS & REPEATS

Many of the songs have some new symbols that you must understand before playing. Each of these represents a different type of ending.

1st and 2nd Endings
These are indicated by brackets and numbers. The first time through a song section, play the first ending and then repeat. The second time through, skip the first ending, and play through the second ending.

D.S.
This means "Dal Segno" or "from the sign." When you see this abbreviation above the staff, find the sign (𝄋) earlier in the song and resume playing from that point.

al Coda
This means "to the Coda," a concluding section in the song. If you see the words "D.S. al Coda," return to the sign (𝄋) earlier in the song and play until you see the words "To Coda," then skip to the Coda at the end of the song, indicated by the symbol: ⊕.

al Fine
This means "to the end." If you see the words "D.S. al Fine," return to the sign (𝄋) earlier in the song and play until you see the word "Fine."

D.C.
This means "Da Capo" or "from the head." When you see this abbreviation above the staff, return to the beginning (or "head") of the song and resume playing.

CONTENTS

LOVE ME TENDER

Words and Music by
ELVIS PRESLEY and VERA MATSON

Additional Lyrics

3. Love me tender, love me dear;
   Tell me you are mine.
   I'll be yours through all the years,
   Till the end of time.

ALL MY LOVING

Words and Music by
JOHN LENNON and PAUL McCARTNEY

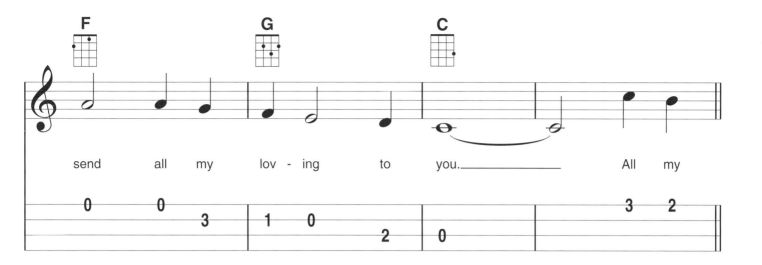

send all my lov - ing to you._____ All my

Chorus

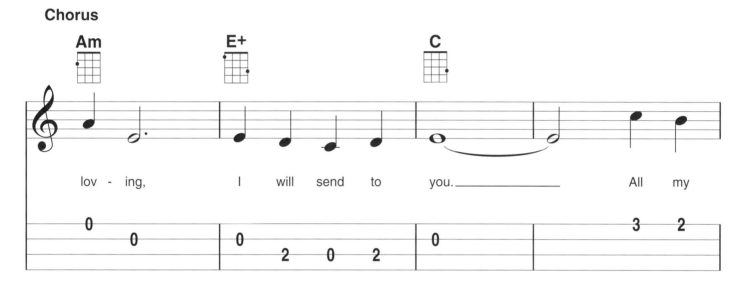

lov - ing, I will send to you._____ All my

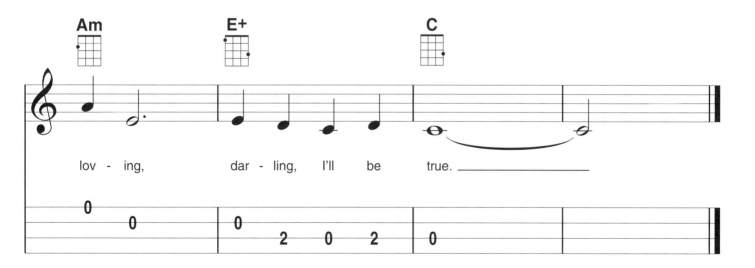

lov - ing, dar - ling, I'll be true._____

Additional Lyrics

2. I'll pretend that I'm kissing the lips I am missing,
   And hope that my dreams will come true.
   And then while I'm away, I'll write home ev'ry day,
   And I'll send all my loving to you.

GOODNIGHT, IRENE

Words and Music by
HUDDIE LEDBETTER and JOHN A. LOMAX

Verse

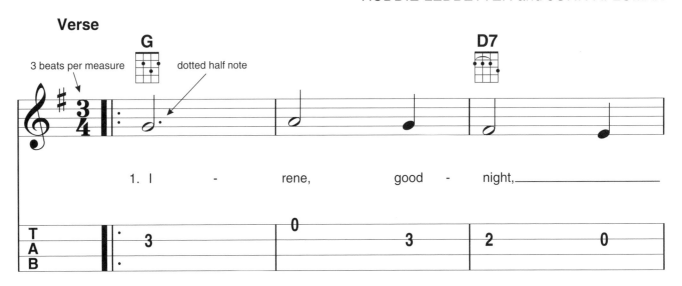

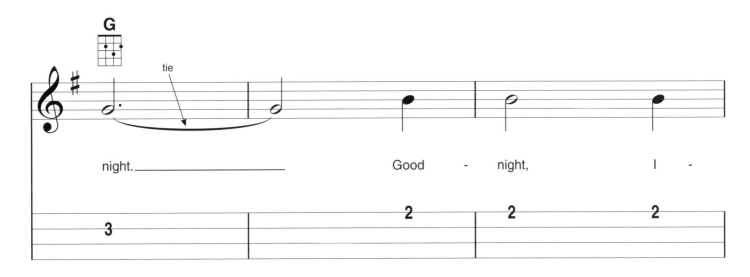

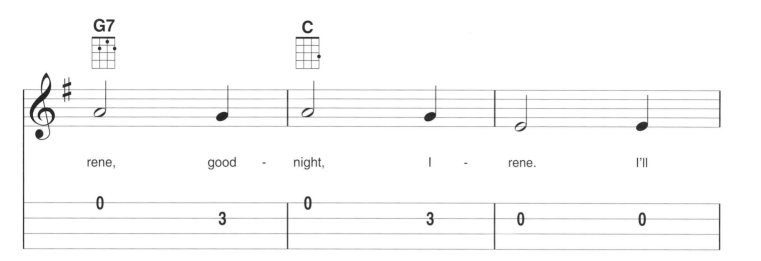

rene,   good - night,   I - rene.   I'll

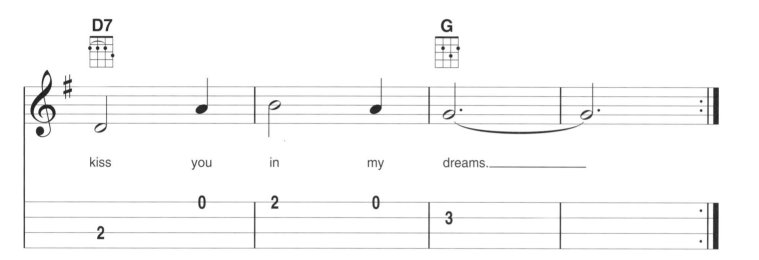

kiss   you   in   my   dreams._____

Additional Lyrics

2. Last Saturday night I got married.
   Me and my wife settled down.
   Now me and my wife are parted.
   I'm gonna take another stroll downtown.

3. Sometimes I live in the country.
   Sometimes I live in the town.
   Sometimes I have a great notion
   To jump into the river and drown.

4. Stop your rambling, stop your gambling.
   Stop your staying out late at night.
   Go home to your wife and family,
   By the fireplace, oh so bright.

LAST NIGHT I HAD THE STRANGEST DREAM

Words and Music by
ED McCURDY

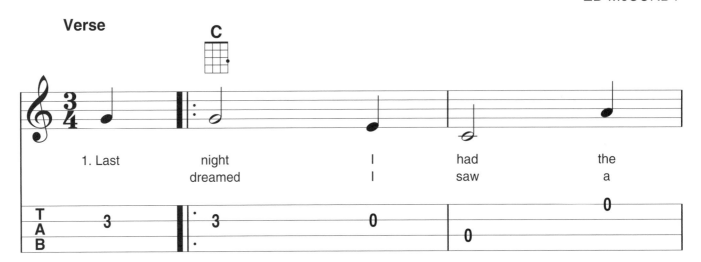

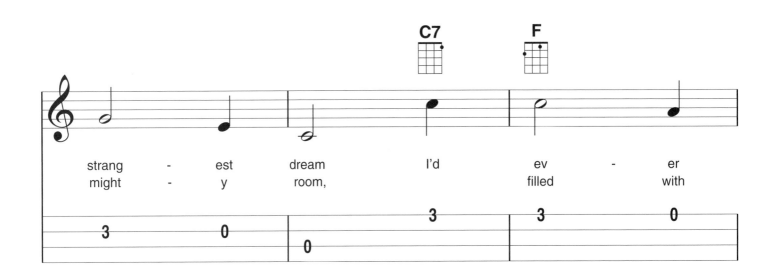

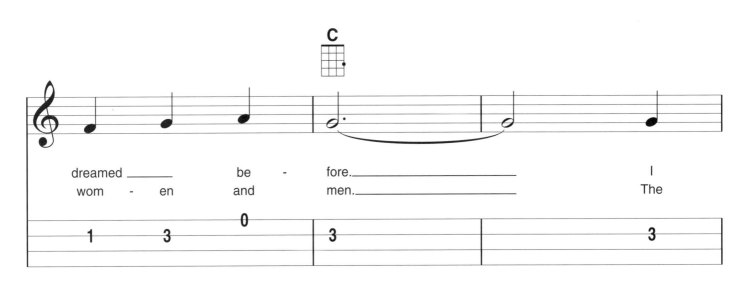

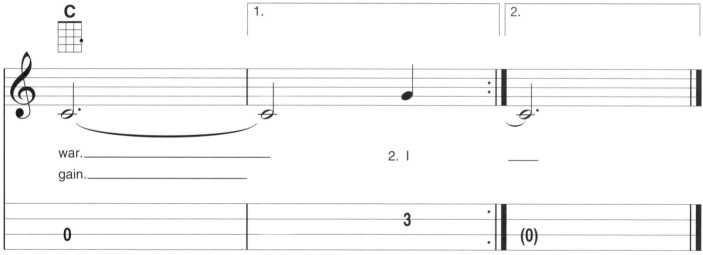

Additional Lyrics

3. And when the paper was all signed,
    And a million copies made,
    They all joined hands and bowed their heads,
    And grateful prayers were prayed.

4. And people in the streets below,
    Were dancing 'round and 'round,
    While swords and guns and uniforms,
    Were scattered on the ground.

PASTURES OF PLENTY

Words and Music by
WOODY GUTHRIE

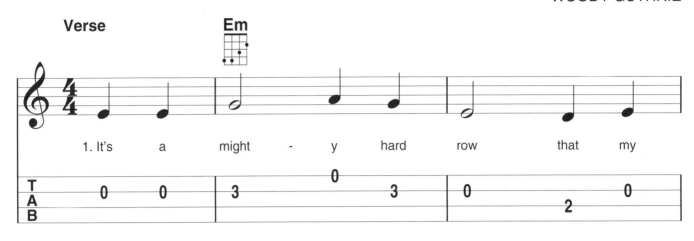

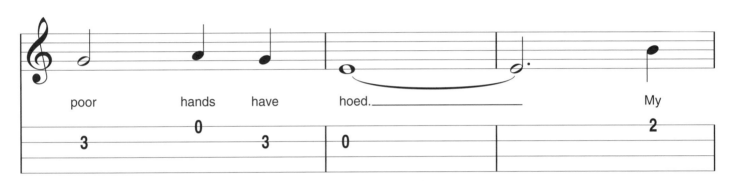

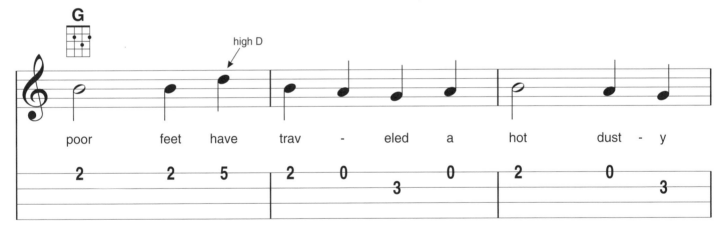

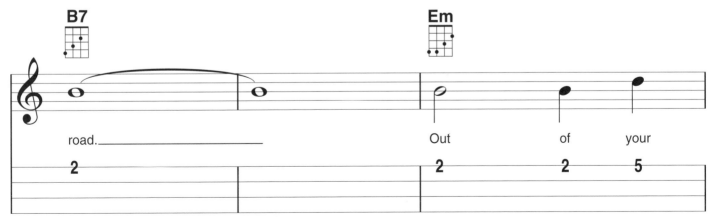

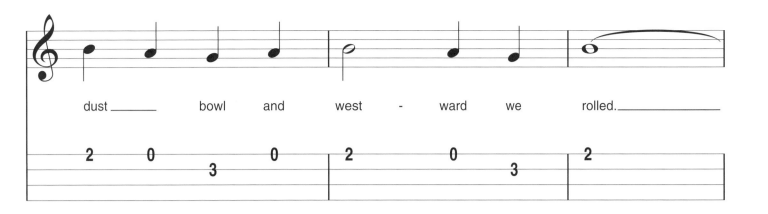

dust _____ bowl and west - ward we rolled._____

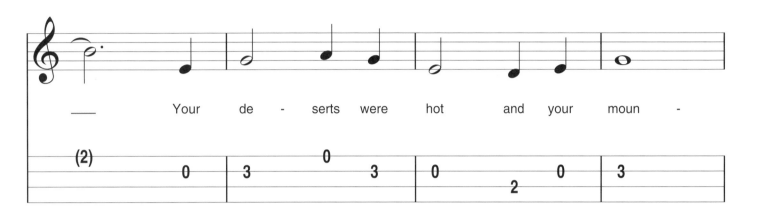

_____ Your de - serts were hot and your moun -

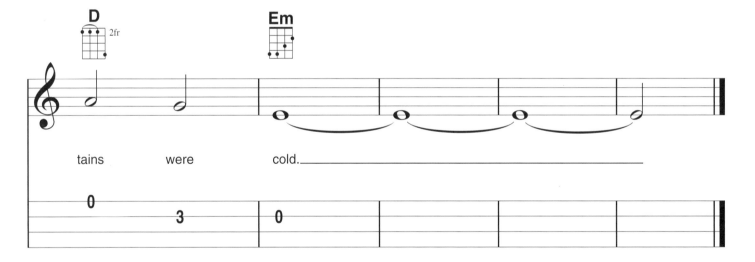

tains were cold._____

Additional Lyrics

2. I've worked in your orchards of peaches and prunes, slept on the ground in the light of the moon.
   On the edge of your city, you've seen us and then, we come with the dust and we go with the wind.

3. California and Arizona, I make all your crops, and it's north up to Oregon to gather your hops.
   Dig the beets from your ground, cut the grapes from your vine, to set on your table your light sparkling wine.

4. Green pastures of plenty from dry desert ground, from that Grand Coulee Dam where the waters run down.
   Every state in this union us migrants have been, we'll work in your fight and we'll fight 'til we win.

5. Well, it's always we ramble, that river and I, all along your green valley I'll work 'til I die.
   My land I'll defend with my life, if it be, 'cause my pastures of plenty must always be free.

I WALK THE LINE

Words and Music by
JOHN R. CASH

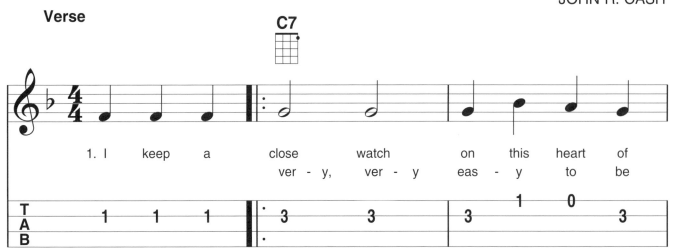

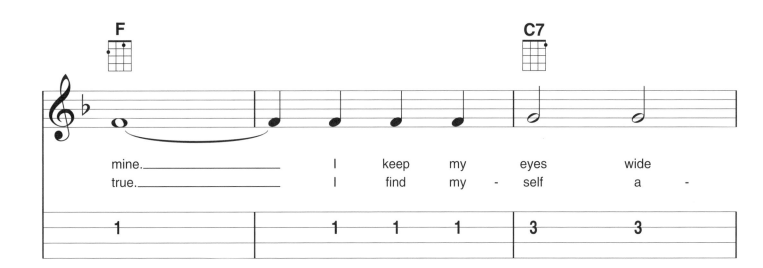

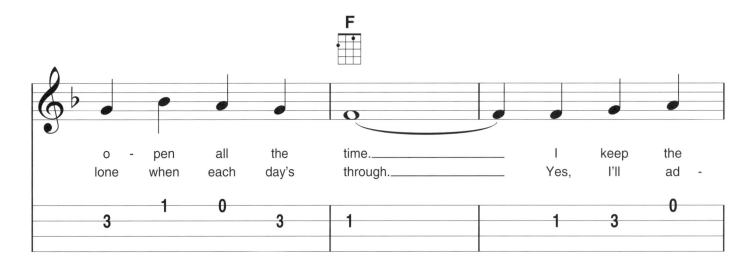

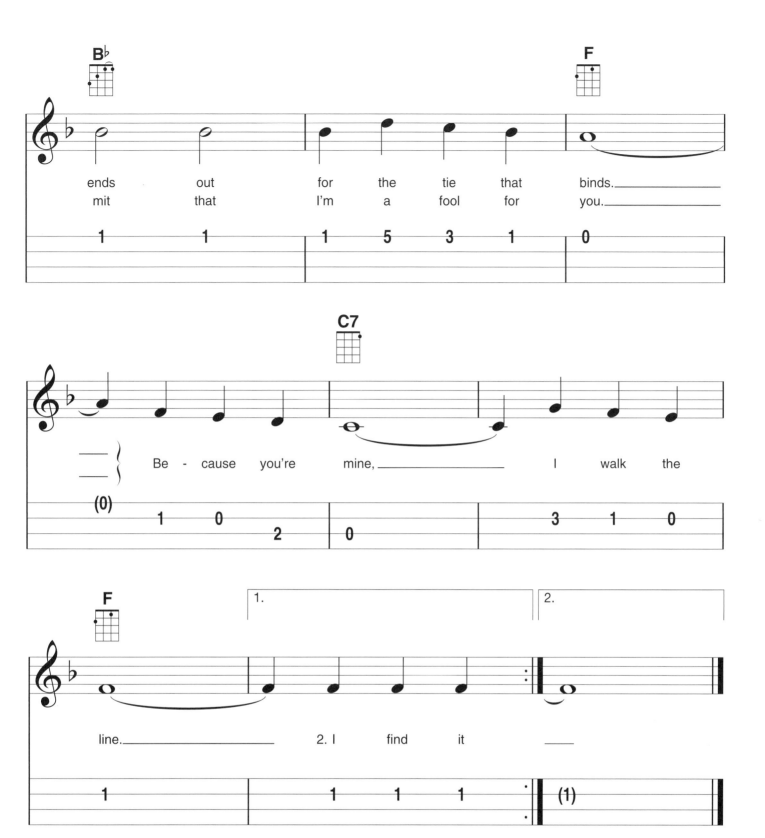

Additional Lyrics

3. As sure as night is dark and day is light, I keep you on my mind both day and night.
   And happiness I've known proves that it's right. Because you're mine, I walk the line.

4. You've got a way to keep me on your side. You give me cause for love that I can't hide.
   For you I know I'd even try to turn the tide. Because you're mine, I walk the line.

5. I keep a close watch on this heart of mine. I keep my eyes wide open all the time.
   I keep the ends out for the tie that binds. Because you're mine, I walk the line.

THE HOUSE OF THE RISING SUN

Words and Music by
ALAN PRICE

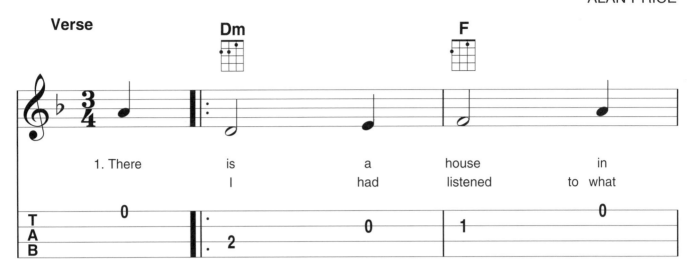

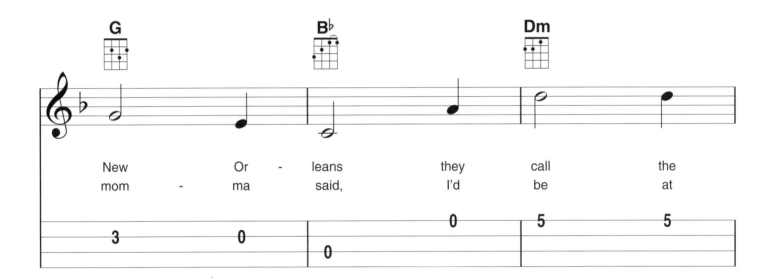

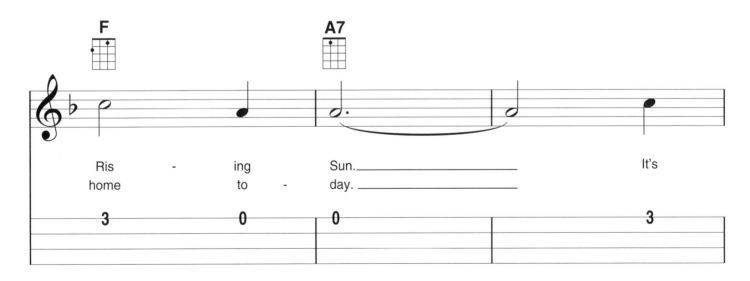

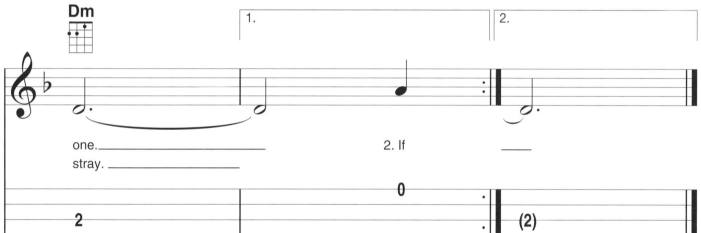

Additional Lyrics

3. The only thing a gambler needs is a suitcase and a trunk,
   And the only time he's satisfied is when he's all a-drunk.

4. Go tell my baby sister never do like I have done.
   To shun that house in New Orleans they call the Rising Sun.

5. I'm going back to New Orleans, my race is almost run.
   Going back to end my life beneath the Rising Sun.

This Land Is Your Land

Words and Music by
WOODY GUTHRIE

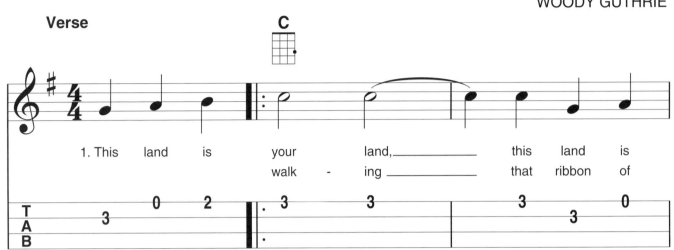

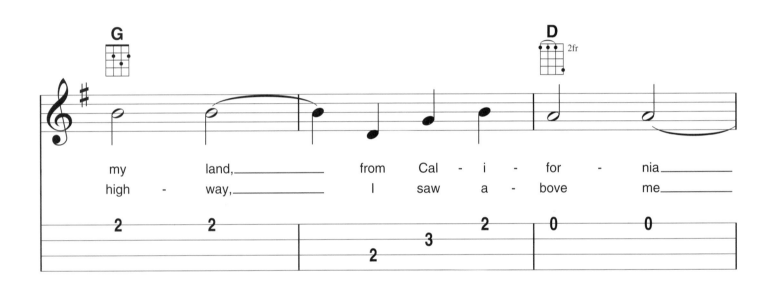

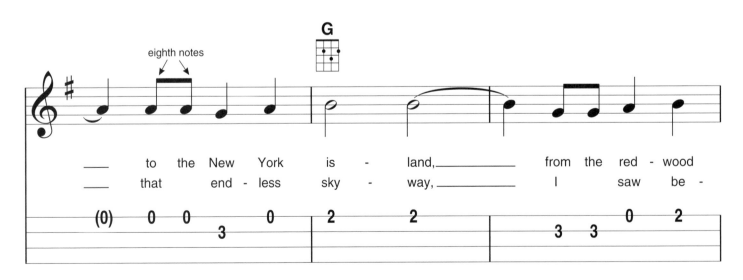

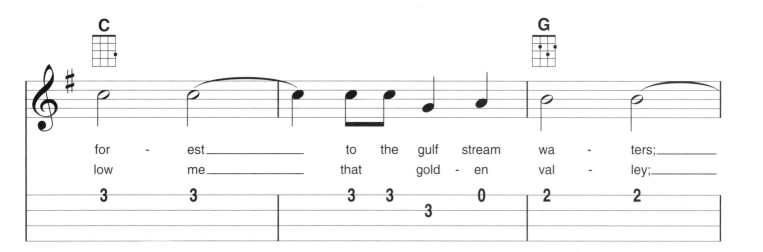

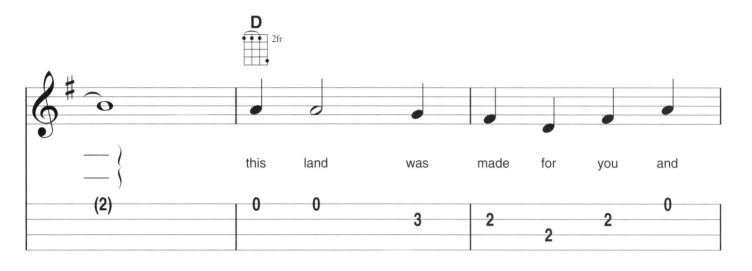

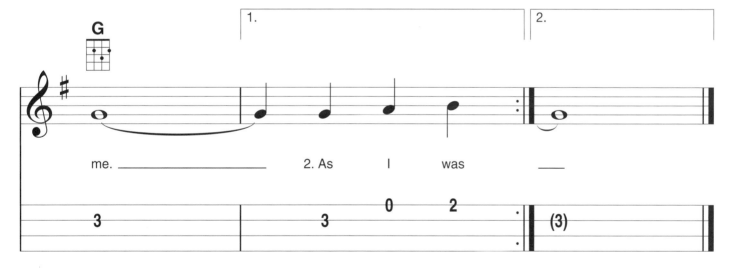

Additional Lyrics

3. I've roamed and rambled, and I followed my footsteps
   To the sparkling sands of her diamond deserts.
   And all around me a voice was sounding,
   "This land was made for you and me."

4. When the sun comes shining, and I was strolling,
   And the wheat fields waving, and the dust clouds rolling.
   As the fog was lifting a voice was chanting,
   "This land was made for you and me."

5. In the shadow of the steeple I saw my people,
   By the relief office I seen my people.
   As they stood there hungry, I stood there asking,
   "Is this land made for you and me?"

6. Nobody living can ever stop me
   As I go walking down that freedom highway,
   Nobody living can ever make me turn back.
   This land was made for you and me.

I'M SO LONESOME I COULD CRY

Words and Music by
HANK WILLIAMS

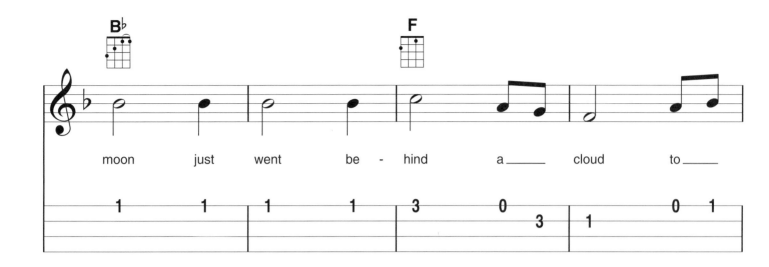

moon just went be - hind a____ cloud to____

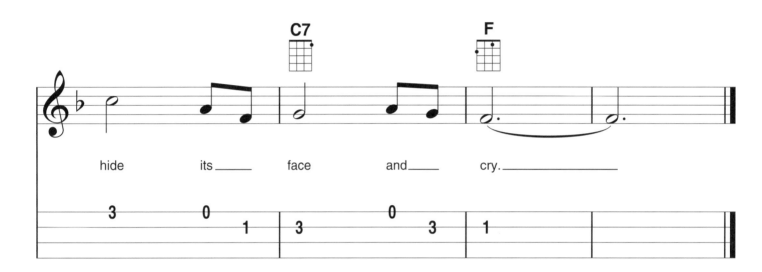

hide its____ face and____ cry.____

Additional Lyrics

3. Did you ever see a robin weep,
   When leaves began to die?
   That means he's lost the will to live,
   I'm so lonesome I could cry.

4. The silence of a falling star
   Lights up a purple sky.
   And as I wonder where you are,
   I'm so lonesome I could cry.

WE SHALL OVERCOME

Inspired by African American Gospel Singing, members of the Food and Tobacco Workers Union,
Charleston, SC, and the southern Civil Rights Movement

Musical and Lyrical Adaptation by
ZILPHIA HORTON, FRANK HAMILTON,
GUY CARAWAN and PETE SEEGER

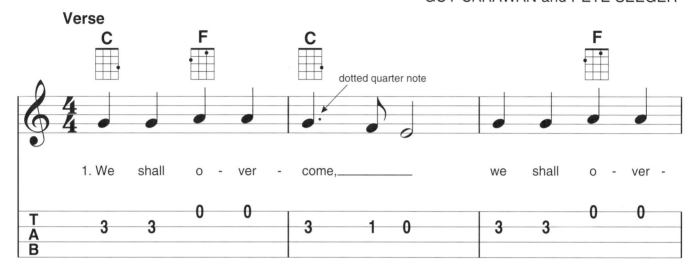

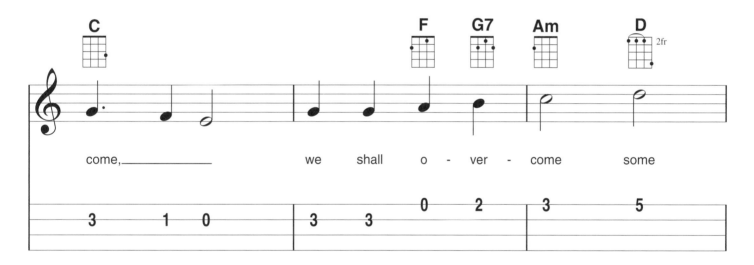

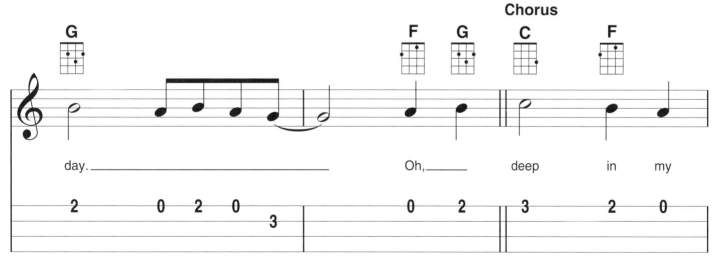

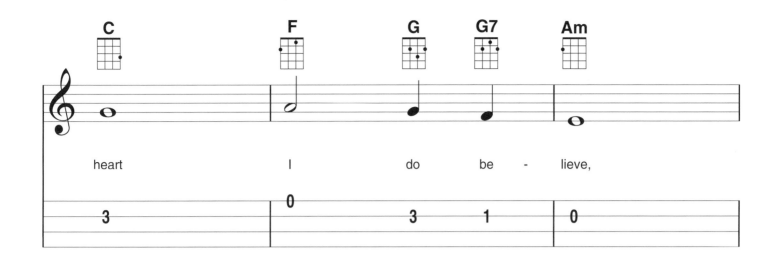

heart   I   do   be - lieve,

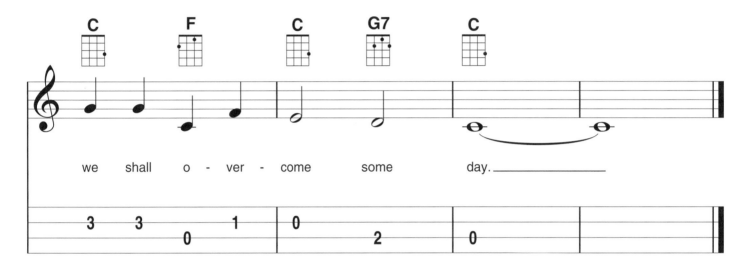

we   shall   o - ver - come   some   day._____

Additional Lyrics

2. We'll walk hand in hand,
   We'll walk hand in hand,
   We'll walk hand in hand some day.

3. We shall live in peace,
   We shall live in peace,
   We shall live in peace some day.

4. We shall all be free,
   We shall all be free,
   We shall all be free some day.

5. We are not afraid,
   We are not afraid,
   We are not afraid, today.

6. We shall overcome,
   We shall overcome,
   We shall overcome some day.

YOUR CHEATIN' HEART

Words and Music by
HANK WILLIAMS

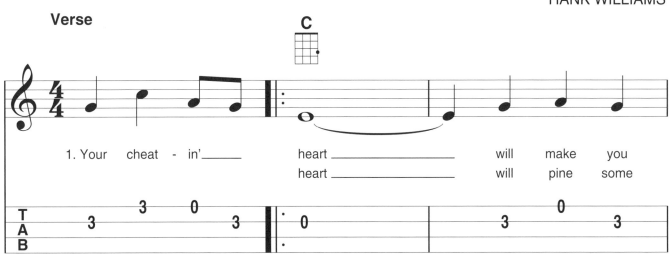

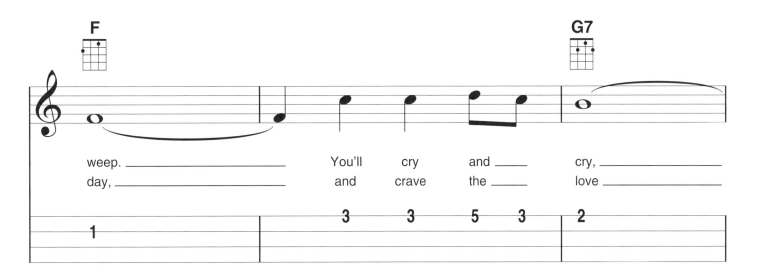

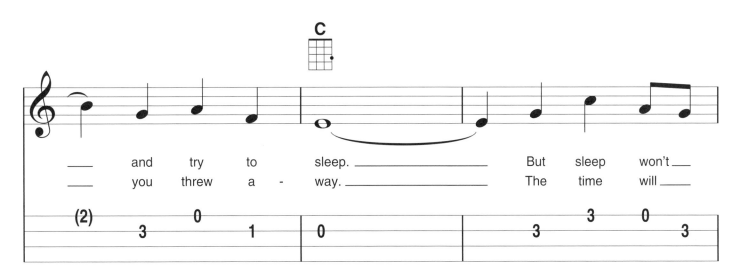

NOWHERE MAN

Words and Music by
JOHN LENNON and PAUL McCARTNEY

Bridge

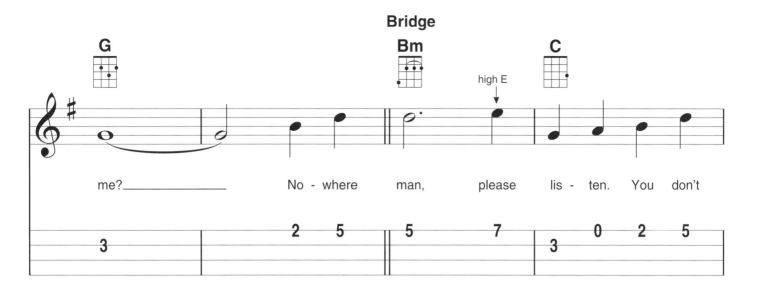

me?_____ No - where man, please lis - ten. You don't

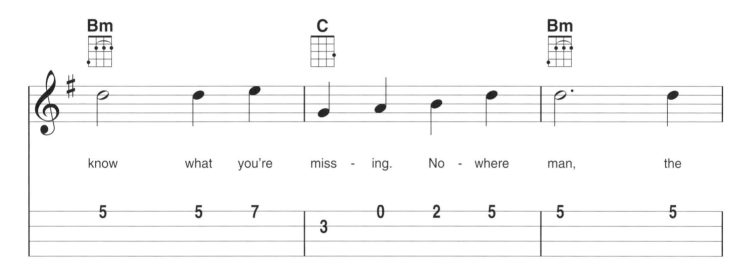

know what you're miss - ing. No - where man, the

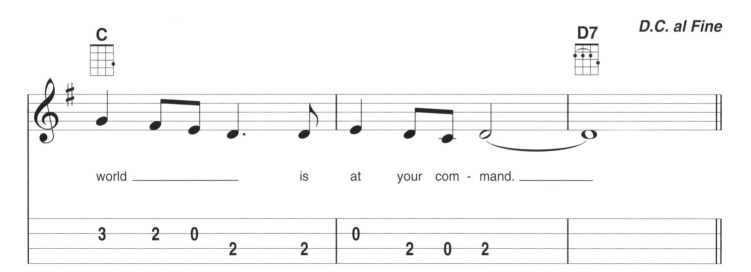

D.C. al Fine

world _____ is at your com - mand. _____

Additional Lyrics

2. He's as blind as he can be, just sees what he wants to see.
   Nowhere man can you see me at all?
   Nowhere man, don't worry. Take your time, don't hurry.
   Leave it all till somebody else lends you a hand.

OB-LA-DI, OB-LA-DA

Words and Music by
JOHN LENNON and PAUL McCARTNEY

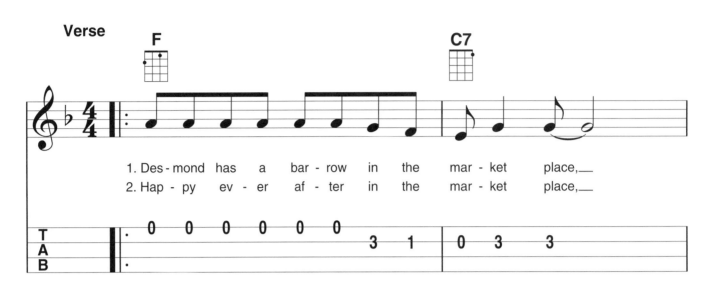

1. Des - mond has a bar - row in the mar - ket place,___
2. Hap - py ev - er af - ter in the mar - ket place,___

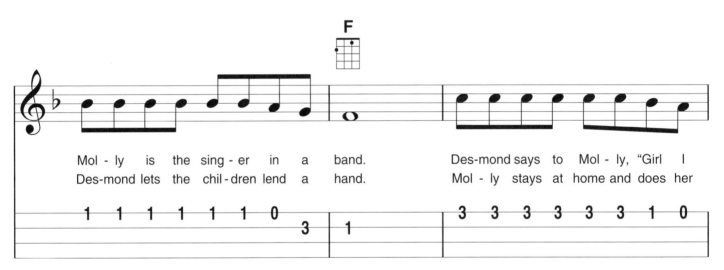

Mol - ly is the sing - er in a band.
Des - mond lets the chil - dren lend a hand.

Des - mond says to Mol - ly, "Girl I
Mol - ly stays at home and does her

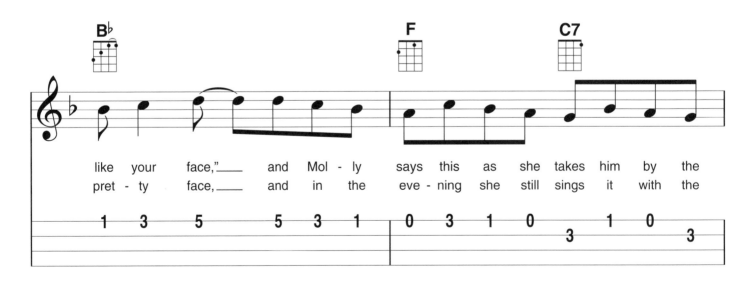

like your face,"___ and Mol - ly
pret - ty face,___ and in the

says this as she takes him by the
eve - ning she still sings it with the

Additional Lyrics

3. Desmond takes a trolley to the jeweler's store,
   Buys a twenty-carat golden ring.
   Takes it back to Molly waiting at the door,
   And as he gives it to her she begins to sing:

4. Happy ever after in the market place,
   Molly lets the children lend a hand.
   Desmond stays at home and does his pretty face,
   And in the evening she's a singer in the band.

HEART AND SOUL

from the Paramount Short Subject A SONG IS BORN

Words by FRANK LOESSER
Music by HOAGY CARMICHAEL

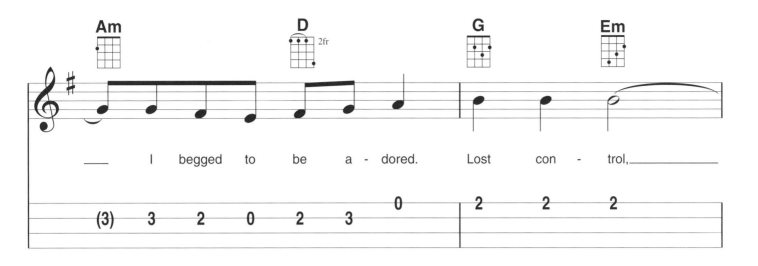

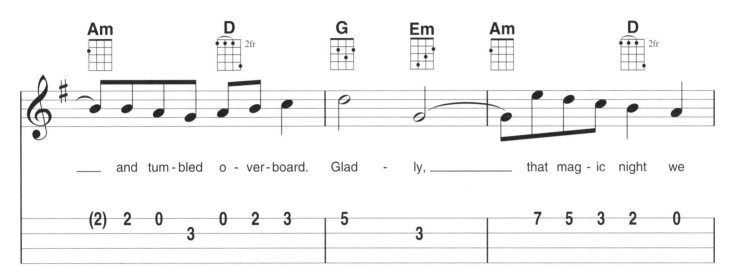

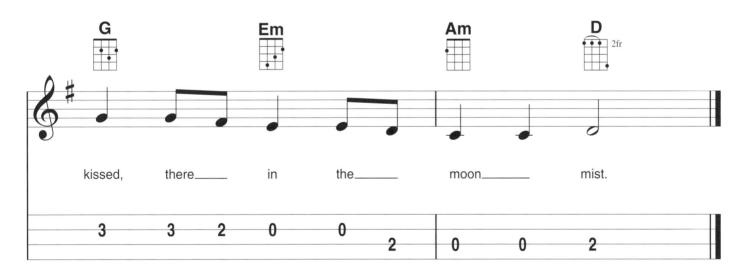

Additional Lyrics

2. But now I see,
   What one embrace can do.
   Look at me,
   It's got me loving you.
   Madly;
   That little kiss you stole,
   Held all my heart and soul.

BLUE EYES CRYING IN THE RAIN

Words and Music by
FRED ROSE

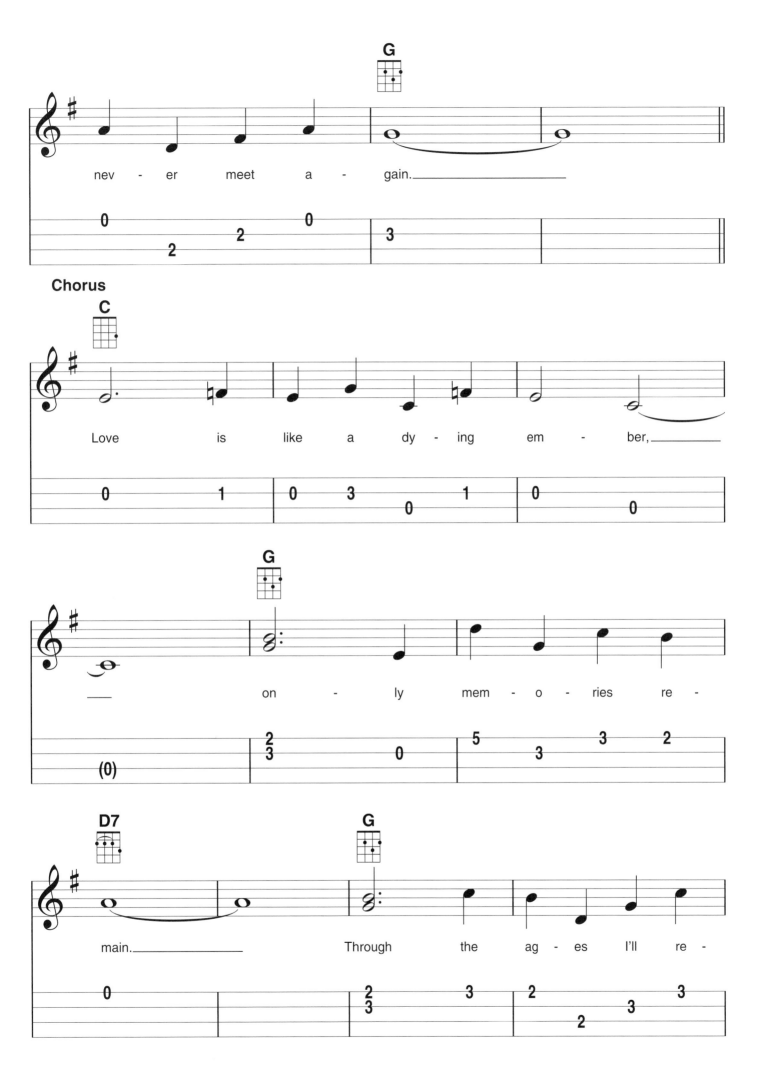

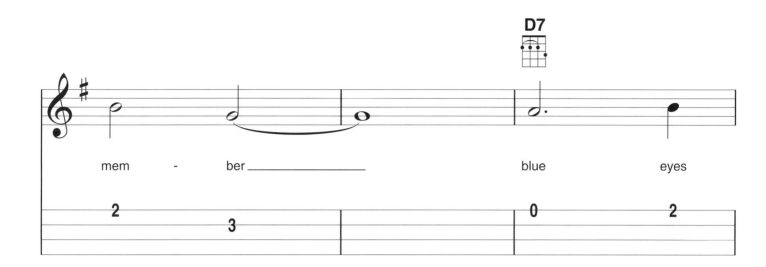

mem - ber _____ blue eyes

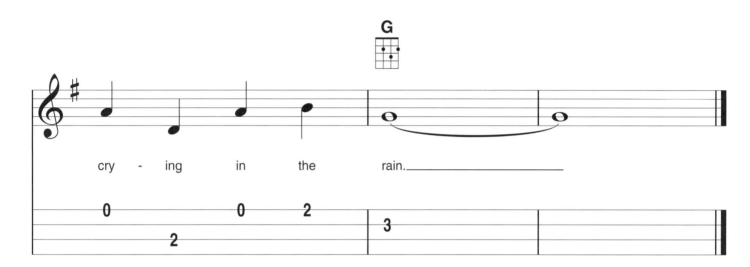

cry - ing in the rain._____

Additional Lyrics

2. Now my hair has turned to silver,
   All my life I've loved in vain.
   I can see her star in heaven,
   Blue eyes crying in the rain.

Chorus: Someday when we meet up yonder,
We'll stroll hand in hand again.
In a land that knows no parting,
Blue eyes crying in the rain.

BLUES SKIES

from BETSY, featured in BLUE SKIES

Words and Music by
IRVING BERLIN

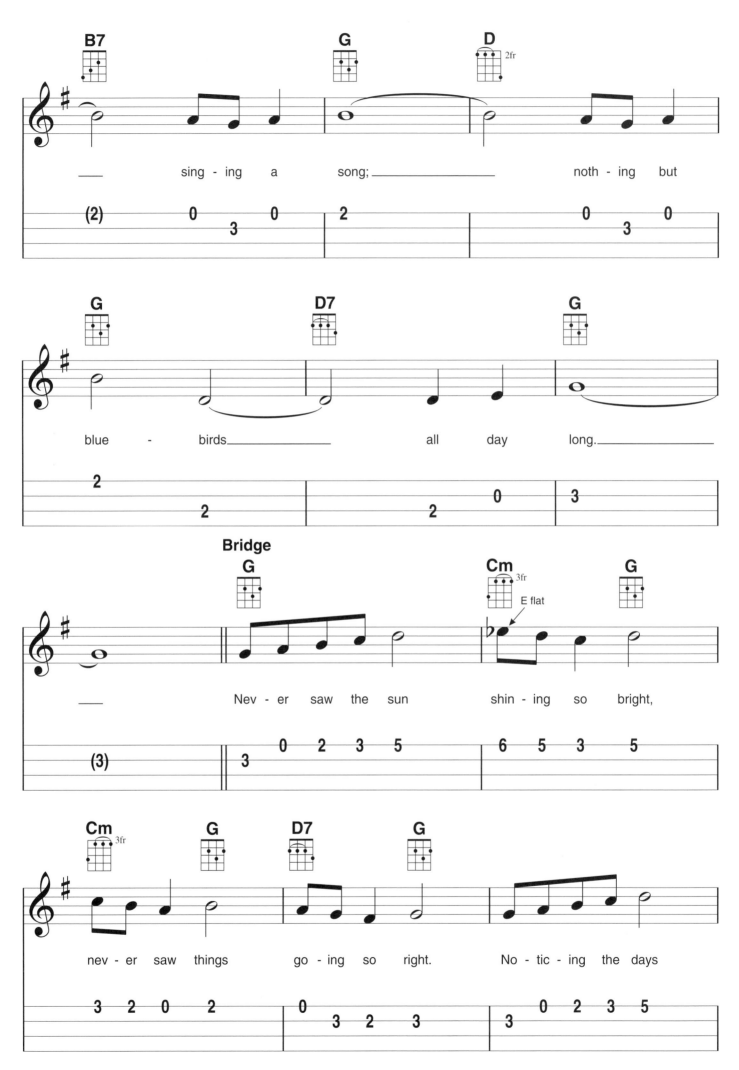

EIGHT DAYS A WEEK

Words and Music by
JOHN LENNON and PAUL McCARTNEY

Verse

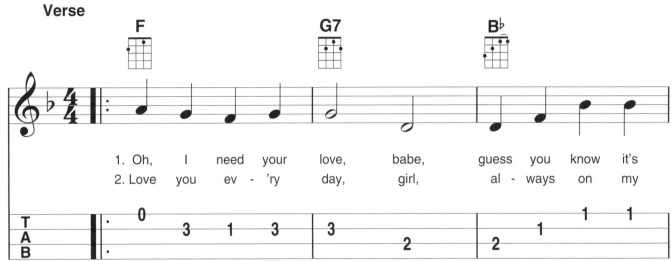

1. Oh, I need your love, babe, guess you know it's
2. Love you ev - 'ry day, girl, al - ways on my

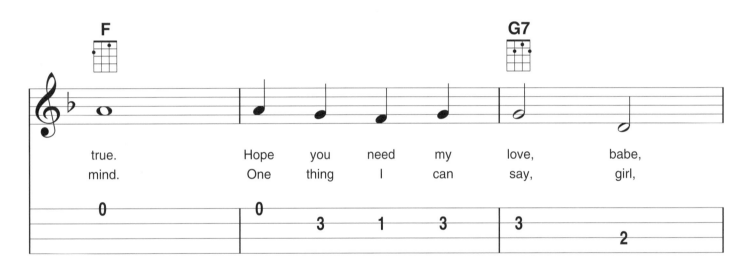

true. Hope you need my love, babe,
mind. One thing I can say, babe, girl,

Chorus

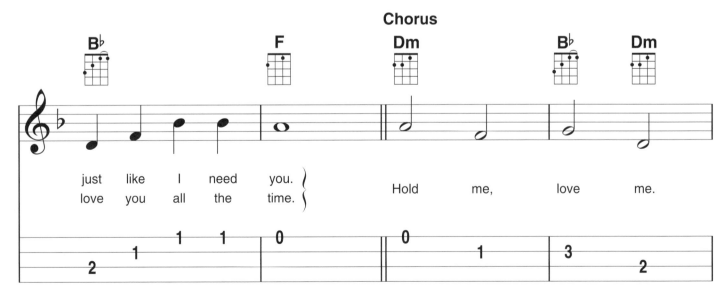

just like I need you.
love you all the time. Hold me, love me.

TOM DOOLEY

Words and Music Collected, Adapted and Arranged by
FRANK WARNER, JOHN A. LOMAX and ALAN LOMAX
From the singing of FRANK PROFFITT

Additional Lyrics

3. Trouble, oh, it's trouble, rolling through my breast.
Long as I'm-a living, boys, ain't-a gonna be no rest.

4. Hand me down my fiddle, play it if you please.
This time tomorrow, it'll be no use to me.

5. If it weren't for Sheriff Grayson, no trouble would I see.
If it wasn't for Sheriff Grayson, I'd be in Tennessee.

6. This time tomorrow, where do you reckon I'll be?
Way down yonder in a hollow, hangin' from a white oak tree.

Blues Stay Away From Me

Words and Music by ALTON DELMORE,
RABON DELMORE, WAYNE RANEY and HENRY GLOVER

Verse
Swing feel

Additional Lyrics

3. Life is full of misery.
Dreams are like a memory,
Bringing back your love that used to be.

4. Tears, so many I can't see.
Years don't mean a thing to me.
Time goes by, and still I can't be free.

YESTERDAY

Words and Music by
JOHN LENNON and PAUL McCARTNEY

Bridge

HAL·LEONARD®
UKULELE PLAY-ALONG

Now you can play your favorite songs on your uke with great-sounding backing tracks to help you sound like a bona fide pro! The audio also features playback tools so you can adjust the tempo without changing the pitch and loop challenging parts.

1. POP HITS
00701451 Book/CD Pack $15.99

3. HAWAIIAN FAVORITES
00701453 Book/Online Audio $14.99

4. CHILDREN'S SONGS
00701454 Book/Online Audio $14.99

5. CHRISTMAS SONGS
00701696 Book/CD Pack $12.99

6. LENNON & MCCARTNEY
00701723 Book/Online Audio $12.99

7. DISNEY FAVORITES
00701724 Book/Online Audio $14.99

8. CHART HITS
00701745 Book/CD Pack $15.99

9. THE SOUND OF MUSIC
00701784 Book/CD Pack $14.99

10. MOTOWN
00701964 Book/CD Pack $12.99

11. CHRISTMAS STRUMMING
00702458 Book/Online Audio $12.99

12. BLUEGRASS FAVORITES
00702584 Book/CD Pack $12.99

13. UKULELE SONGS
00702599 Book/CD Pack $12.99

14. JOHNNY CASH
00702615 Book/Online Audio $15.99

15. COUNTRY CLASSICS
00702834 Book/CD Pack $12.99

16. STANDARDS
00702835 Book/CD Pack $12.99

17. POP STANDARDS
00702836 Book/CD Pack $12.99

18. IRISH SONGS
00703086 Book/Online Audio $12.99

19. BLUES STANDARDS
00703087 Book/CD Pack $12.99

20. FOLK POP ROCK
00703088 Book/CD Pack $12.99

21. HAWAIIAN CLASSICS
00703097 Book/CD Pack $12.99

22. ISLAND SONGS
00703098 Book/CD Pack $12.99

23. TAYLOR SWIFT
00221966 Book/Online Audio $16.99

24. WINTER WONDERLAND
00101871 Book/CD Pack $12.99

25. GREEN DAY
00110398 Book/CD Pack $14.99

26. BOB MARLEY
00110399 Book/Online Audio $14.99

27. TIN PAN ALLEY
00116358 Book/CD Pack $12.99

28. STEVIE WONDER
00116736 Book/CD Pack $14.99

29. OVER THE RAINBOW & OTHER FAVORITES
00117076 Book/Online Audio $15.99

30. ACOUSTIC SONGS
00122336 Book/CD Pack $14.99

31. JASON MRAZ
00124166 Book/CD Pack $14.99

32. TOP DOWNLOADS
00127507 Book/CD Pack $14.99

33. CLASSICAL THEMES
00127892 Book/Online Audio $14.99

34. CHRISTMAS HITS
00128602 Book/CD Pack $14.99

35. SONGS FOR BEGINNERS
00129009 Book/Online Audio $14.99

36. ELVIS PRESLEY HAWAII
00138199 Book/Online Audio $14.99

37. LATIN
00141191 Book/Online Audio $14.99

38. JAZZ
00141192 Book/Online Audio $14.99

39. GYPSY JAZZ
00146559 Book/Online Audio $15.99

40. TODAY'S HITS
00160845 Book/Online Audio $14.99

HAL·LEONARD®
www.halleonard.com

Prices, contents, and availability subject to change without notice.

1021
483